This book is dedicated to those who suffered and died from illegal abortions and to our daughters and granddaughters, whose lives depend on the ability to make reproductive choices safely and legally.

Choices

A publication of The NARAL Foundation

Karen A. Schneider, Editor

copyright © 1997 by The NARAL Foundation

All rights reserved.

ISBN 0-9662262-0-8

A note to our readers

We invite you to experience the lives of the one dozen women in this book as they make the intensely personal and profound decision about abortion. After you have read their stories, please go back and read the historical narrative that places their experiences in the broader struggle for reproductive rights in the United States. The narrative begins on page 9 and continues across the bottom of each page.

Preface

by Anna Quindlen

Anna Quindlen is a Pulitzer Prize-winning columnist, novelist and mother of three. Her work has appeared in America's leading newspapers and magazines and on the fiction and non-fiction bestseller lists. A Fellow of the Academy of Arts & Sciences and a Member of The NARAL Foundation Board of Directors, Anna is an influential voice for a woman's freedom to choose.

In 1973, when I was a college dormitory counselor, I was asked by a terrified young woman to find a place where she could have an abortion. The mission, it turned out, required me merely to walk into the office of the student health service, where I was given the telephone number of a clinic. So my story lacks drama, except for two elements. The first was the reaction of a senior who was a counselor in another dorm and who had a friend who became pregnant in high school. You have no idea, she said fervently, and a bit bitterly, how lucky all of you are.

The second drama, of course, was the one that was taking place within the heart and mind of the freshman who was having the abortion.

It is now a quarter century later; I have talked during the course of my work as a columnist to dozens of women like the ones whose stories are contained in this book, women who have been pregnant and who have ended their pregnancies. I have read reams of case law, spoken with legislators and lobbyists, ricocheted from one secondary issue to another as the landscape of abortion rights in this country has changed.

And yet I learned everything I really needed to know the very first time the issue touched my life. There would always be, above all, the human pain, confusion, and ultimately resolve that I found within that young woman who asked for my help so long ago. And behind that, a bulwark, would be the law and the past, the past that made women who had lived it indelibly aware of the legislative privilege that was the birthright of those of us of a certain age. They and their friends had flown to foreign countries, swallowed strange medicinal concoctions, paid off medical students, gone away to give birth and then to give away the babies they had not wanted and now mourned. We made appointments and went to clinics. It was the difference between one decade and another. It was the difference between night and day.

There are alive in America today several generations of women who have never known a nation in which it was not legally permissible to end a pregnancy. It might be difficult to have an abortion, that's for sure, in counties where there were no clinics, in states where parents had to give permission. It might even be close to impossible, if they were poor and the price of the procedure was high.

But those women have always known that the choice was there, that the price of an unwanted pregnancy could be, for them, counted in dollars and not in lost fertility, covert childbirth, or forced marriages. They could talk about abortion with their friends, as something people they knew did, had done, not as some black secret, to be admitted years later with whispers and choking sobs. There is a chasm between generations, between those young women who came of age thinking of abortion as a medical procedure, and those who knew it as a crime.

That chasm is marked by the Supreme Court decision that may be the only one most Americans know by name. *Roe v. Wade* has been attacked for its legal reasoning as well as its philosophical underpinnings, for how it divided up the seasons of human gestation and how it divided, continues to divide, perhaps will always divide, this nation.

But the dividing line it laid down for millions upon millions of American women was more personal than that. *Roe* was the demarcation between one way of living and another.

It didn't make abortion simple, or easy, or automatic. There are still many women who reject the notion of ending a pregnancy. There are still many who choose to end one sadly, with great regret. There are plenty who find an abortion difficult to obtain, for one reason or another, and difficult to live with, too. But easier to live with than the alternatives that marked the lives of their mothers, and grandmothers.

It was true: when I went with that young woman to the clinic, neither of us had any idea how much the ground of privacy and liberty was shifting beneath our feet. We knew only that something cataclysmic had happened in her life and that she was dealing with it the best way she knew how. It was her decision to make, and she made it. Legal briefs have been written, debates held, bills drafted. But that's what all of it has always come down to, in the end. Her decision to make, and she made it. Within her own heart and mind and within the law as well.

Introduction

by Karen A. Schneider

"Few decisions are more personal and intimate, more properly private, or more basic to individual dignity and autonomy, than a woman's decision — with the guidance of her physician and within the limits specified in Roe *— whether to end her pregnancy. A woman's right to make that choice freely is fundamental."*

— U. S. Supreme Court Justice Harry Blackmun

Thornburgh v. American College of Obstetricians and Gynecologists

The landmark *Roe v. Wade* decision, delivered a quarter century ago on January 22, 1973, ushered in one of the most profound and sweeping changes for women in the nation's history.

Overnight, illegal abortions were relegated to the history books. There were no more coat hangers, knives, hoses and other instruments of the back alleys. No more hospital wards filled with victims of botched illegal abortions. No more panic and desperation for millions of women who faced unplanned pregnancies. And no more forced childbearing for those who couldn't find or afford an illegal abortion.

Roe was both a gateway to the future and a door slammed shut on the past. It was an indictment of old ways, an apology to those who suffered and died, and a vindication of efforts to repeal the old abortion laws. *Roe* was a triumph for those who believed that the right to choose abortion is central to women's dignity and autonomy.

Twenty-five years ago, it was difficult to predict the impact of *Roe* on women's lives. But the significance of the decision soon became clear: the ability to decide when to bear a child — and when not to — is essential for women's full emancipation and participation in society. Without the freedom to choose, women's march toward equality would have stalled long ago.

For a quarter century, millions of women have grown up under the protection of *Roe*, secure in the knowledge that the freedom to choose is a fundamental American value, a cardinal principle, and a constitutionally protected right.

But is that right secure? From the day *Roe* became law, those who oppose a woman's freedom to choose have worked to undermine it. They have filed legal briefs, enacted legislation, and used intimidation and violence at the clinics.

They have chipped away at the right through state laws such as mandatory waiting periods and parental consent and federal restrictions such as bans on insurance coverage of abortion and abortion funding for low-income women. Opponents of choice also have shifted public attention from the woman to the fetus and the procedure itself, effectively silencing the voices of women who have grappled with the abortion decision. (The history of *Roe* and of reproductive rights in the U.S., as well as the anti-choice backlash, are described more fully in a narrative that appears across the bottom of these pages.)

As Justice Blackmun wrote in his dissent in *Webster v. Reproductive Health Services* in

1989, "For today, at least, the law of abortion stands undisturbed. For today, the women of this nation still retain the liberty to control their destinies. But the signs are evident and very ominous, and a chill wind blows."

This book is an effort by The NARAL Foundation to elevate the voices of women and underscore the importance of reproductive choice to a woman's life, family and future. These personal stories continue a tradition begun by The NARAL Foundation in 1985 with its *Silent No More* campaign, in which women across the nation spoke publicly about their abortion experiences.

The women who tell their stories here carefully evaluated the circumstances of their lives and chose abortion. Some had safe, legal abortions, while others suffered society's disrespect for their choices and disregard for their safety.

Illegal abortions nearly cost Lynn Kahn, Polly Bergen and Mary Roper their lives. Lynn, then a divorced mother of two, was raped one night on her way home from work. After her abortion, she nearly bled to death before finding a hospital that would treat her. As a young actress, Polly desperately wanted to hide the evidence that she had been a "bad girl;" the abortion almost killed her and left her unable to bear children. Mary, a college student, endured four illegal abortion attempts before the pregnancy was terminated; she later began hemorrhaging and had an emergency D&C.

Some women were mothers who faced difficult personal circumstances and chose abortion out of responsibility to their children. NARAL's President Kate Michelman was a young mother in 1970 when her husband abruptly left her. She soon discovered that she was pregnant with her fourth child and sought a hospital abortion. She had to convince a hospital panel of physicians that she was "unfit" to be a mother and endure other indignities. Only three years later, women's health activist Byllye Avery, then a young widow with two children, found herself pregnant but, thanks to *Roe*, was able to have a safe, legal abortion without suffering such humiliation.

Virtually all the women who had legal abortions faced obstacles imposed by opponents of choice. Mary Conley and Krista Reuber endured a gauntlet of protestors. Shannon Lee Dawdy faced mandatory biased "counseling" and a 24-hour waiting period.

And then there is Becky Bell, the Indiana teenager who fell victim to a parental consent law. Afraid to disappoint her parents, Becky had an illegal abortion and died from complications one week later. Her story is told by her mother Karen.

Every woman I interviewed for this project agreed to come forward to help defend the freedom to choose by giving voice to the human dimension of abortion. Some were composed as they told their stories; others choked back tears. Some have told their stories publicly before; others are courageously revealing their experiences for the first time.

"By telling my story, I hope that there will be a greater awareness of the consequences of abortion becoming illegal again," Mary Roper told me. "There will be scared young girls like myself who will end up on kitchen tables or in seedy motels. I don't want anybody to go through what I did."

Karen Bell and her husband, Bill, have long spoken publicly about their tragedy in an effort to help other teenage girls. Karen told me that talking about Becky is a comforting reminder that "Becky was real, and she lived and breathed, and she was mine."

This book is for the Becky Bells of the world and the countless women who died before her. And it is for future generations of women who must be able to exercise the freedom to choose safely, securely and with dignity.

POLLY BERGEN

Polly Bergen is an award-winning stage, screen and television actress, singer, author, businesswoman and public speaker. Born in Bluegrass, TN, in 1930, Polly began her career at age 15 as a nightclub singer. Polly won an Emmy for best actress for her appearance in CBS-TV's "The Helen Morgan Story," and was nominated twice for her role in the ABC miniseries "Winds of War" and "War and Remembrance." During what is now called "the golden age of television," Polly made more than 200 TV appearances and had her own show, "The Polly Bergen Show." She also founded a multi-million dollar mail-order cosmetics company and, more recently, became the chief operating officer of Chantal Pharmaceutical Corp. Polly is a mother and grand-mother, and lives in Beverly Hills and New York City.

Not long after Polly moved to Hollywood in her late teens, she became pregnant and had an illegal abortion. It would have devastating consequences when Polly married and was ready to have children.

When I got my menstrual period, I thought I had hurt myself riding a horse — that's how little I knew about my body. My mom never discussed anything personal like that with me. My parents came from a very poor Southern Baptist background and were not well educated. My father could not read or write. My mother only went through the third grade.

All I knew about sex was that 'good' girls didn't get pregnant unless they were married and 'bad' girls did. I loved my mom and dad dearly, and I felt that getting pregnant without being married would have been the most evil thing I could have done to them. I never wanted them to think that I was a bad girl. I was extremely responsible, well behaved, devoted and willing to do anything to please my parents. I wanted and needed their love and approval more than anything in the world, and I always got it.

In my senior year of high school, I sat down on the back porch with a girlfriend and she told me how you made a baby. I hadn't a clue — and I'd been working as a nightclub singer since I was 15. I had the appearance of a woman in her 20s, so no one ever told me anything because I looked as if I already knew everything.

I was 17 the first time I had sex. As ludicrous as it may sound, I did not even know that I had had sex. In those days, you were supposed to limit yourself to heavy petting because you had to be a virgin when you got married. I didn't know that there had been penetration because I still had my clothes on. When I got home, I realized that something serious had happened because the evidence was there. It was a blow emotionally and psychologically

Throughout U.S. history, a woman's fundamental right to choose has never been fully realized. In the nation's early years, midwives performed abortions up to the point of "quickening" — when fetal movement could be felt — in the fourth or fifth month of pregnancy. In the mid-19th century, the American Medical Association, seeking to consolidate its control over women's health care and diminish competition from mid-

to lose my virginity that way, but eventually I got past it and moved on.

After graduating from high school, I moved to Hollywood to start a career in show business. Shortly thereafter, I began my first serious relationship, which I naively believed would culminate in marriage. This time, I knew I was having sex, but I never thought about getting pregnant because that only happened to bad girls. I didn't know about condoms or diaphragms. Was I ever stupid!

One day, I told my roommate that my breasts seemed larger and my waistband felt tighter than usual. She insisted that I go to her doctor. I had never been to a gynecologist, and it was an upsetting experience. Of course the results of the pregnancy test were even more upsetting. I was terrified and horrified. I started to ask around very quietly, saying I have a friend who is in serious trouble.

I couldn't admit to my parents or anyone except my roommate that I was pregnant. I felt so guilty. The thought of my parents' disappointment and the terrible betrayal of their trust in me was devastating. That was all I thought about. It didn't occur to me that I wasn't prepared emotionally or financially to care for a child.

The man I was involved with was an entertainer who was on a European tour. I had no idea when he would return, but I had come to the realization that marriage was definitely not on his mind. The most important thing for me was to hide the fact that I had been a bad girl. For me, there was no other choice.

Someone gave me the phone number of a person who did abortions and I made the arrangements. I borrowed about $300

from my roommate and went alone to a dirty, run-down bungalow in a dangerous neighborhood in east Los Angeles. A greasy looking man came to the door and asked for the money as soon as I walked in. He told me to take off all my clothes except my blouse; there was a towel to wrap around myself. I got up on a cold metal kitchen table. He performed a procedure, using something sharp. He didn't give me anything for pain — he just did it. He said that he had packed me with gauze, that I should expect some cramping, and that I would be fine. I left.

The whole experience was terrifying. I was terrified in the car all the way downtown, I was terrified knocking at the door, I was terrified when I saw him, and I was terrified of being alone with him in his house. But when you're dealing with something that is so imperative, you just grit your teeth and say, 'If this is the way it has to be, then this is the way it has to be.'

I walked back to the car and cried for about a half hour. At home, as I fixed myself some soup, I started to have stomach pains and to bleed quite profusely. I lay down and went to sleep, hoping that when I woke up the pain would be gone. When my roommate came home from work at two or three in the morning, she found me laying in a pool of blood. She got me dressed because I couldn't function; I was in excruciating pain. She said she was taking me to an emergency room. I begged her not to because the doctors would know what had happened.

The doctors stopped the bleeding and sewed something up inside me. Of course, they knew what had happened because I was packed with gauze. I was so ashamed.

wives and others, campaigned to criminalize abortion. By the turn of the century, abortion was a crime in

every state. It even was illegal to dispense or provide information about birth control.

States, however, did not vigorously enforce the criminal abortion statutes until the end of World War II,

when an intense effort to elevate childbearing and motherhood as women's primary role coincided with

One doctor told me that if my friend had not arrived when she did, I would have simply bled to death.

They gave me some blood transfusions, and I remained in the hospital for three days. It took me a year to pay that medical bill off. I did my best to put the experience behind me until I discovered that I could not bear children.

In my first and second marriages, I had several miscarriages. I desperately wanted a child and went to see a fertility specialist. During my second marriage, I had an ectopic pregnancy that ruptured the fallopian tube. My doctor said I had so much scar tissue that he was amazed I could get pregnant at all.

After my second ectopic pregnancy, which they caught in time, they reconstructed the damaged fallopian tube. Then I had a third tubular pregnancy, which they did not diagnose correctly, and the fallopian tube ruptured again.

By the time they got me into surgery, I had lost a great deal of blood. While I was in the operating room, the surgeon went out to tell my husband that he wanted to perform a partial hysterectomy. He said it was obvious I could never carry a baby to term because there was so much damage, and he believed I probably wouldn't survive another tubular pregnancy. My husband gave his permission. I was only 33 years old.

Today I have two adopted children, a stepdaughter, and three grandchildren. My children were adults before I revealed the truth about my abortion. It happened quite by chance.

It was a week before a big pro-choice march on Washington in 1989, and I had been asked to speak for NARAL at a mother-daughter luncheon on behalf of choice. I invited both my daughters to come with me. As I began to speak, I suddenly found myself revealing the story of my abortion. The truth just poured out of me. I broke down. Both of my daughters broke down. It was so powerful and emotional for them because it made them understand their place in my life and how valuable they were to me.

I don't think I could ever have told that story to anyone if my mom or dad were still alive.

Today, when I speak about choice, I never portray the other side (the nonviolent ones) as being wrong, because they are not. They are people who believe very strongly in their views on choice, as I do mine.

When anti-choice people approach me, I tell them that the government doesn't belong on either side of this issue. I also say that if the government has the power to pass a law saying you can't have an abortion, then the government also has the power to say that you must have an abortion. When you put that kind of argument in front of an anti-choice group, they get it, although of course they don't necessarily change their position.

The government should never have a choice regarding a woman's right to choose. It is a choice that should be made personally by a woman with her husband, her family, her priest, her minister, her rabbi, or just within her own heart. In the end, a woman has to decide what is the right choice for her at that moment in time. If you can't trust a woman with a choice, how can you trust her with a child?

stricter enforcement of abortion laws. Many women who had entered the workforce as part of the war effort were forced out as returning soldiers reclaimed their jobs. Public support for women's paid labor waned. Women married at a younger age than ever and birth rates soared. A woman's role now centered entirely on her family.

LYNN KAHN

Lynn Kahn is a counselor and Community Affairs Liaison at the Hope Clinic for Women in Granite City, IL. The clinic provides reproductive health care services to women. She has three grown children and five grandchildren.

In 1964, Lynn, then a divorced mother of two toddlers, was raped by a man as she left work. She became pregnant and almost died from the illegal abortion.

I was 24 years old and was living in St. Louis with my two children, who were two and three years old. I had recently divorced and was the sole supporter of my children. I worked in an office during the day and at a bar at night to provide for my family.

One evening on my way home from work, a man raped me in an alleyway. I was so ashamed and angry, but I didn't go to the police. In those days, when a woman brought charges of rape, she was put on the defensive more than the man who raped her. Your whole credibility as a woman was questioned. I was afraid that they would say it was my fault for working in a bar in the first place. I realize now that it wasn't anything that I did, but back then it was different. I had two small children, and I didn't want to risk losing them.

I got pregnant. I was still in shock from the rape and then to find out that I was also pregnant was pretty hard.

Of course back then abortion was illegal. My only thought was I can't — I won't — have this fetus. I couldn't consider carrying a product of a rape inside my body for that length of time. But I didn't know anything about abortion. It just wasn't talked about. I asked someone who played in the band at the bar, and he told me that he might know someone who could help me. It was one of those cases of someone-who-knows-someone-who-knows-someone who would get in touch with me at some point. It took a long time — it was almost four months before a woman called to say she would do the abortion. It seemed like an endless amount of time.

I scraped together $300 by saving some and borrowing the rest from friends without telling them the real purpose of the loan. I called a girlfriend and said that I had a date and might be gone for the evening. She agreed to take care of my children and keep them overnight.

The woman came to my apartment. She didn't ask if I wanted to know how the abortion would be done — and I didn't want to know. I just knew I didn't want to be pregnant anymore.

In the 1950s, hospitals created review boards to evaluate the validity and reasonableness of a woman's request for therapeutic abortion. These generally all-male panels delved into a woman's sexual and marital history and passed moral judgment on her behavior. Increasingly, the committees denied women access to therapeutic abortion.

She asked me to lie down on the bed. She took a long rubber orange tube out of a bag, put it in one of my kitchen pans, filled it with water, and boiled it on the stove to sterilize it. When it was cool enough for her to touch, she inserted the tube in me, and told me to lie on my back for the next 24 hours. She said that she would come back to my apartment the next morning to remove the tube and see if everything was alright.

It struck me all of a sudden that she might not come back. I was afraid, and prayed that she would come back. I told myself to get a grip and that I could pull the tube out if I had to. I tried not to panic, but I was cramping and hurting. I thought I was going to die.

I reached for a pad and pencil and wrote a will. I didn't have much, just a ring and a few other possessions, but I wanted to make sure that my children would have my things. I wrote a letter to each of them saying that I loved them and that I was sorry. I put the letters next to the bed.

I listened to the radio and continued to pray. To my surprise, the woman came back the next day. She said that she was going to remove the tube and I would probably have some bleeding. It wasn't painful, but then the blood started to come out fast. Her eyes got really big, and she left quickly.

I lay there for a minute. I felt as if my blood and my life were running out of me all at once. I knew I was going to die.

I called another girlfriend and told her what had happened. She and her boyfriend rushed over. He picked me up and ran down three flights of stairs. We drove to the nearest hospital. The woman at the front desk could see that I was bleeding heavily, and she asked if I had an abortion. I told her I hadn't. Then she asked me whether I had health insurance and when I said that I didn't, she said, 'I believe it's an abortion and we're not going to take you here.'

We got back in the car and raced clear across town to City Hospital. I was so afraid that we wouldn't make it in time. I felt guilty that the woman in the first hospital knew that I had an abortion, and I felt like a leper that nobody wanted. I didn't know what to expect when I got to City Hospital.

Thankfully, they took me immediately

Women's loss of autonomy in making reproductive decisions according to their individual needs and beliefs led to increased demand for illegal abortion. Each year, an estimated 250,000 to one million women sought abortions despite their illegality. Some women found qualified physicians whose concern and compassion for women's health and lives led them to risk their medical licenses and livelihood to provide

Lynn Kahn

to the emergency room and hooked me up to an IV. The doctor asked whether I had an abortion, and I said I hadn't. He kept telling me that it looks like an abortion and I kept telling him that it wasn't. He insisted it was and said that he had to notify the police.

He told me, though, that I had an extremely bad infection and that he would treat me. They gave me blood transfusions. Before he put me to sleep, he said again that he was going to notify the police. I cried and finally admitted that it was an abortion and said I had two small children and, please, could he have mercy on me?

While I was asleep, they did a D&C. I woke up in a ward with other women. At the opposite end of the ward, a police-woman stood near a woman who was handcuffed to her bed. I realized that this was the ward where bad people go. I thought that the police would come to handcuff me at any moment.

I was so frightened. I didn't want to talk to anybody, didn't want to ask questions, didn't want to cause any attention to be focused on me.

I spent four terrified days in the hospital.

Someone talked to me about paying the bill, and I said I couldn't. They asked me if I could call three or four friends to donate blood to pay back the blood they had given me; my friends obliged. Meanwhile, I waited and waited and waited, but the police never came.

When it was all over, I was thankful to be alive and glad that I didn't have that pregnancy inside me anymore. I moved away and started life over. I never talked about the abortion until I started working at the clinic in 1986, 22 years later.

I was talking with our director of counseling and it all came out. It was such a big relief — I felt like concrete blocks were lifted off my shoulders. It was the beginning of my being able to heal fully. I no longer had to keep this shameful thing locked inside.

It struck me then that I never thanked the doctor for saving my life and not calling the police. I am deeply sorry for that. I know now what he risked. Working here is my way of saying thank you, a chance to pay back what he gave me — my life.

abortions. Some women chose to travel to Puerto Rico, Mexico and Sweden to obtain abortions.

Still others were forced to turn to untrained and unscrupulous providers who took advantage of women's desperation and profited from their despair. Some women were blindfolded and driven to secret locations, where they underwent dangerous procedures under unsafe and unsanitary conditions. Women

MARY ROPER

Mary Roper works as a management consultant, and has traveled widely throughout the United States, Canada, Europe, Asia, Australia, and South America for her business. Mary, 48, is married and has a stepdaughter. Mary became pregnant while in college in 1968; her story is about one woman's determination to terminate her pregnancy and the indignities and risks to her life that she suffered during her difficult quest for an abortion.

I was 19, a sophomore at a Midwest university, and rather naive. I was not sexually active or a frequent party goer. One evening, I went to a college party with a boy I was dating; his name was Tim. I drank some punch that tasted like cherry pop. I remember going upstairs and passing out in a bedroom. When I woke up, Tim was on top of me. I got up, went to the bathroom, and saw that I was bleeding. I knew I was no longer a virgin. I felt embarrassed and ashamed.

It took me a long time before I could admit to myself that I had been raped. Initially, I felt that I was responsible for what happened because I had gotten drunk. It would take me years of working through my guilt, shame, and anger to be able to say, 'It was not my fault. I was raped.'

I continued to see Tim and have intercourse with him on a regular basis. I didn't have the self-esteem and support to stand up and say 'no' to an unhealthy, abusive relationship.

I ended up getting pregnant. I didn't consider having the baby because of the shame it would have brought to my family and to me. I was born and raised Catholic and had attended an all girls' Catholic high school. I felt that there was no way that I could be a single mom in our community. I was distraught, scared, and feeling guilty. I knew that abortion was illegal, but I was determined to have one.

Tim encouraged me to have the abortion. He was dating other women and did not want me to bear his child. The experiences that I went through attempting and finally getting an abortion are something you read about, something that happens to other women. Well, it happened to me, and this is my story.

I got pregnant in early summer. I had a job working at the University Extension Center, and I told one of my co-workers that I was pregnant and wanted an abortion. She said that she had a friend who could help. I called in sick one day and drove three hours to see her friend. I went alone — and I was scared.

The woman lived on a street of tidy bungalows. Her house was neat and orderly, and the woman, who was a little older than me, looked respectable and clean. She was also kind, and realized that I was frightened. She offered me liquor to calm my nerves.

poured into hospitals with life-threatening internal injuries and infections caused by coat hangers, tubes, and chemicals. Many women died.

The illegality of contraception ensured continued high rates of unplanned pregnancy and the need for abortion. Contraception did not become legally available to married couples until 1965, when the Supreme

"I was one of the lucky ones.

I survived; others did not."

I refused, and she proceeded. I got up on her kitchen table, and she inserted a coat hanger in me.

At that moment, I became numb — numb to any physical, emotional, mental or spiritual pain. Had I allowed myself to feel anything, I might have gone over the edge. I deadened the pain by shutting down. When she removed the coat hanger, I got dressed and drove home.

I kept waiting for something to happen — to bleed, to have cramps. But nothing happened.

Tim got the name of a man in town who could help. I went on my lunch hour to a seedy motel, the kind you can rent by the hour; today it is boarded up and deserted. I found the room number that he had given me. The man was overweight and unkempt, and he smelled of cigarettes. He repulsed me.

He had a hose, similar to the kind people used for enemas, which he used on me. I paid him, left, and went back to work. Again, I was numb to pain. And again, there were no results.

My co-worker's friend came to town. We arranged another meeting. She made a second attempt with the coat hanger. Once again, nothing happened. I was getting more and more desperate.

I contacted the man from the seedy motel. He agreed to make a second attempt with the hose. I brought Tim with me, and he waited in another room. I started to get ready for the procedure, but I sensed that something was different this time. I still remember the smell of his breath and the look on his face as he started to unzip his pants. I was so overcome with fear; I thought I was going to throw up. I managed to scream, and

Tim came in the room. The man zipped himself up, grabbed his bag and left.

As I was living this nightmare, Tim was telling friends in town that I was pregnant and seeking an abortion. One day, two police officers came to see me. They said they heard that I was pregnant and looking for an abortion. I lied and said it wasn't true. They asked me to call them if someone offering an abortion tried to contact me, and they left. I became scared and depressed.

Tim heard about a dentist in a nearby city who performed abortions. We went to see him. He said I was too far along, and refused to help me. At this time I was about four weeks pregnant.

Tim then found someone in Chicago. We drove three hours and went to an agreed-upon meeting place at a Burger King. A car was waiting for us. We were blindfolded, put in the backseat, and driven somewhere. When they took our blindfolds off, we appeared to be in a doctor's office — there were medical school diplomas on the walls and surgical equipment in the room. I felt I was finally going to get help.

The doctor and nurse were compassionate, gentle and understanding. The doctor numbed my vaginal area and performed a suction type of abortion. He gave me medication to lessen the possibility of hemorrhaging and told me to take it easy. We paid him, were blindfolded again, and taken to our car. We drove home.

The next morning, I didn't feel any pain or cramping. I was tired and scared, but also relieved. Maybe it was finally over.

A few weeks later, I was getting ready to return to college. As I was leaving, my parents said they heard I was pregnant.

Court, in Griswold v. Connecticut, *recognized the constitutional right of married couples to use contraceptives; the Court's* Eisenstadt v. Baird *decision in 1972 extended that right to unmarried individuals.*

In the late 1950s, segments of the medical, legal and religious communities began urging the liberalization of abortion laws. The American Law Institute, for example, a respected professional organization of

Was it true? I could honestly say, 'No, I am not pregnant.' I remember their relief — and my own.

A couple of months after the abortion, as I was working on a term paper, I began to hemorrhage. My roommates took me to the campus health center. An ob-gyn examined me, and said I needed an emergency D&C. First, he needed my parents' written permission and got in touch with them immediately. They gave their approval in a Western Union telegram. I had the D&C.

At a follow-up visit, the doctor handed me some birth control pills and told me to use them. He must have known what happened to me. But he never accused me and never passed judgment. For that, I was grateful.

Believe it or not, I kept seeing Tim. That was my low self-esteem at work. At the same time, I felt shame and guilt, and I was fearful that people would find out. What would they think of me? Would I be shunned? Would they think I was immoral or evil? Would my friends still be there for me? I became seriously depressed and suicidal.

I went to see a Catholic priest, who threw me a life ring. I needed to hear that I was not a bad person and that I was forgiven. He was sympathetic and said that God forgave me and I needed to forgive myself. He also said, 'Mary, you have so much to give and so much life in you. Stop hanging around people who are waiting to die.' The priest gave me hope and helped me see that I was a good person.

By the time I was 23, I knew I needed therapy. I had been having nightmares about the rape and abortions. Even today, more than 30 years later, I still have an occasional nightmare.

I made progress in my therapy and had a big breakthrough four years ago. I was working with a spiritual counselor. We talked about the abortion and how it still haunted me. She said, 'whatever is still there, let's bring it into the light and pray that whatever needs to be healed will be healed.'

At home, 20 minutes later, I had excruciating shooting pains in my stomach. I broke out in a full-body cold sweat. I couldn't move. I lay on the floor. I was hyperventilating, and my hands and arms were becoming numb.

I started to breathe deeply and to pray. I prayed that the pain would pass. I prayed for an end to the nightmare. I realized that I was experiencing the physical pain of all the attempted abortions that I had never allowed myself to feel. I was releasing three decades of stored up pain. And then it passed.

When my husband came home, he wanted to take me to the hospital. I told him that I didn't think they would find anything wrong. Later, I had a physical exam to make sure I was in good health, and they found nothing wrong.

It has been quite a journey, one that I hope no woman ever has to experience again. Why tell my story after so many years? Why now?

It is my hope and prayer that the right to choose will never be taken away. And these days it seems a possibility.

We must have the freedom to make reproductive choices and access to counseling and support. Looking back, I can say that despite my experiences, I was one of the lucky ones. I survived; others did not. I tell my story for them, so that no woman will ever have to repeat my journey.

legal scholars, judges and attorneys, revised the widely accepted Model Penal Code to permit abortion in cases where the pregnancy threatened the woman's physical or mental health, the fetus was impaired physically or cognitively, or the pregnancy was a result of rape or incest. By 1970, 12 states had liberalized their abortion laws along these lines.

CAROL WALL

Carol Wall is Vice President for Development and Public Affairs at Pathfinder International, a family planning organization based in Boston. Carol's experience with an illegal abortion led her to pursue a career in reproductive health. She has served as Executive Director of Planned Parenthood organizations in Ohio and Pennsylvania and as a NARAL Board Member. Carol has been married for 40 years and has three grown children. Carol was a young mother when she became pregnant again in 1966. Determined to terminate the pregnancy, Carol traveled to Puerto Rico to look for an abortion.

Our first child was a "honeymoon baby" — she was born nine months and one day after our wedding. I was barely 22. The shock of an unplanned pregnancy hit me very hard. I was in the middle of my graduate education when my first child was born. Though I loved her very much, I was very disappointed not to be able to finish nursing school, and I could never go back.

Although we used birth control, it wasn't reliable, and we had four children in six years. My third child, a girl, was born with microcephaly, a condition that left her severely retarded and without human responses. She lived in an institution and died when she was four.

My husband and I had a warm, loving family. But we were under some financial strain and burdened by the nonstop chores and logistics of caring for a large family. When I became pregnant for a fifth time in 1966, it was extremely clear to me that, financially and emotionally, I could not have another child. My responsibility for my children was total and overwhelming, and I felt that one more child would push us over the edge. Even though abortion was illegal, I was absolutely determined that I would not have this baby. My husband, Duncan, agreed with me.

I started calling around. I talked with Dr. Robert Hall, who was active in the abortion reform movement in New York. He said that he couldn't give me specific information, but that if I went to Puerto Rico, I could find a safe, although illegal, abortion. My gynecologist was supportive but had no information; later, I would give him the name and phone number of the physician who helped me, and he gave it out countless times.

I resolved to go to Puerto Rico. It was a big risk. I didn't speak Spanish. I didn't know if I would find someone who could perform an abortion. I didn't know what I would find there at all. But I felt that there was no other choice.

The involvement of prominent religious leaders lent credibility to the abortion reform movement. In 1967, two dozen Protestant and Jewish clergy established the Clergy Consultation Service, an organization that grew to include thousands of clergy, including some Catholic priests. Religious leaders referred women to doctors who could perform safe abortions in Puerto Rico, Great Britain and even in the States.

We took out a loan from the credit union to buy the plane ticket and pay for the abortion. I wasn't frightened. I was calm and I felt powerful. I was finally taking control of my life and making a decision that was right for me and for my family. When I arrived in San Juan, I felt that my mission was somehow out of sync with the lush landscape and tropical weather. But I was undeterred.

At my hotel, the first thing I did was open the yellow pages. I found a few listings in English, like 'Women's Doctor.' I tore out the page. I got in a cab, pointed to the first listing, and we were off. The taxi stopped at a university medical school. I walked down a shaded walkway and into a stucco building.

The doctor's office was crowded with women who looked ready to deliver at any minute. The receptionist seemed to know why I was there. She gave me a disapproving look and quickly ushered me into the doctor's office.

I told the doctor why I had come to see him. He cursed at me in English and said, 'You American women are terrible. You come to Puerto Rico to break the law. You think we're going to take care of your sins.' After about five minutes of this insulting talk, I said, 'I didn't come all this way and leave my husband and children at home to be yelled at by you. I will not be treated this way. Now, can you tell me how I can have an abortion?' He said, 'No, get out of my office.' I was furious.

I found a cab, pointed to the next name on my list, and managed to explain that I wanted him to wait for me. By the third stop, he must have realized what was happening because he gave me a knowing look. Sure enough, I had come to the right place.

The stucco building was tucked away in a semi-residential neighborhood and it had no windows — just right for a clandestine procedure. The cramped waiting room was filled with women who did not look very pregnant. Several of them had obviously come long distances.

A man named Dr. Garcia examined me. He was very old and his hands shook. I thought, 'What have I done?' He confirmed that I was about six weeks pregnant. The nurse told me to come back the next morning with $800 in cash, to come alone and to

At the same time, the modern women's movement began raising consciousness about women's role in society.

Growing numbers of women entered the workforce, where some employers used pregnancy as a justification

for discriminatory employment practices. As women expanded their societal roles, they soon recognized that

control of their reproductive lives was critical to their continued progress and advancement. Feminist leaders

Carol Wall

leave my luggage behind so that I wouldn't attract attention. It was very cloak-and-dagger. But I was too relieved to care.

Back at the hotel, I wrote a long letter to Duncan and the children in case I didn't survive the abortion. I told them how much I loved them and asked them to understand the importance of what I had done. I cried as I wrote and prayed that they would never receive the letter. This was a low point for me because I had to face the possibility that I might die.

I addressed the envelope to Duncan and placed it on top of my suitcase with a note asking the hotel manager to mail the letter if I did not return.

I woke up early the next morning and rushed over to the doctor's office. Several other women were already there. I was anxious about the general anaesthesia they would give me for the D&C. I didn't like losing control; I had done everything else very deliberately. But I never wavered in believing that I was doing the right thing.

I was taken fairly quickly into the operating room which, I was relieved to see, looked like a real operating room with medical equipment and bright lights.

The doctor with the shaky hands had a son, and fortunately the younger Dr. Garcia performed the abortion; he looked more dependable and seemed kind. Not much was spoken; their English was as limited as my Spanish.

When I woke up, it felt wonderful to be alive. I was not bleeding heavily. I stayed in the recovery room for about two hours; they came in to check my vital signs, which were okay. I got dressed and left.

The magnitude of what happened hit me when I got back home. I felt that I had undergone a profound experience. I felt so badly because my husband had been suffering. He had not heard from me because we wanted to avoid the expense of a long-distance phone call. My husband suffered much more than I did — and he suffered in silence because we had to keep this secret. We had — and still have — such love for each other; to have an act of love turn out this way was so terribly sad.

About seven years later, *Roe v. Wade* was handed down. It was one of the most wonderful moments of my life. I had such a feeling of freedom — it was like a release from slavery.

gave voice to these beliefs and worked to repeal the abortion laws. Meanwhile, a case involving the constitutionality of a Texas anti-abortion statute was working its way through the courts.

Sarah Weddington and Linda Coffee, Texas attorneys and advocates of women's rights, had filed a lawsuit challenging the state's 100-year-old criminal abortion law on behalf of a young woman known

Becky Bell

BECKY BELL

Becky Bell lived with her parents, Karen and Bill, and brother in a small town near Indianapolis, IN. Becky was a junior in high school in 1988 when she became pregnant. She sought an abortion at a women's health clinic but learned that, under Indiana law, she first had to obtain the consent of one parent. Afraid to disappoint her parents, Becky had an illegal abortion and died from complications one week later. This is Karen Bell's story.

Becky and I were very close. She was an easy child, gentle and innocent. I would worry sometimes about my son, Billy, but never about Becky. She loved horses, music, school and life itself. When Becky was 16, she began dating a friend of Billy's. She was crazy about him. He was a rebel and completely different from her, but that's who she loved.

Soon after Becky turned 17, I noticed that she seemed quieter than usual. One evening she asked to go to a party on the south side of town. I said, 'Becky, I don't want you to go to the south side, it's not safe there.' I had a feeling that something wasn't right, but my son said, 'My God, Mom, let Becky go. You protect her too much, and she's been sad lately.'

I let her go.

I was laying awake in bed waiting for her to come home. At 12:45 in the morning, I heard her trying to open the door. She was crying, and said, 'Mom, it was a horrible party. I feel like I've got the flu like Dad.' Beck never lied; I never doubted what she said. I told her to go to bed and she would feel better in the morning.

But she did not. After school on Monday, she still felt sick. By Wednesday she had a fever of 104 and a strange cough. I told her we were going to the doctor. She turned white. She said, 'Mom, oh Mom, please, oh please, I don't want to go. Just give me some aspirin, I'll be okay, please, please.'

She was nearly hysterical, so I respected her wishes. Later I realized that she feared the doctor would discover the abortion and tell us about it. And later he said that he would have.

On Friday, September 16, she said she would go to the doctor. She was so weak that my husband and I had to carry her to the car. The doctor sent us immediately to the hospital. We put her in the backseat and she asked me to sit next to her. I held her close.

The nuns and nurses at St. Vincent Hospital, where we have taken her for everything, kept asking Beck, 'What have you done to yourself?' I heard the nurses say her veins had

collapsed. They put oxygen on her, but Becky pulled the mask off. I leaned down and said, 'Honey, tell Mom, tell me, honey.' She said, 'Mom, Dad, I love you, forgive me.' And that was it. Her heart stopped.

They said that her lungs had literally come apart from infection, and they hooked her up to life support. We called our family to come to the hospital. Billy was away at college and couldn't make it in time. Late that night, with grandma, grandpa, and other relatives gathered, the doctor said, 'We don't know if we can save the baby.' And I thought, 'The baby? My God, Becky was pregnant.' At 11:29 that night, the doctors said that there was no hope and took her off life support.

Bill and I went home. I don't know where Billy went. I don't know where anybody went. There are no words to describe how Bill and I felt. We just kept saying, 'Oh my God, my baby, oh my God.'

The coroner performed an autopsy and called us. 'Your Rebecca Suzanne died from an illegal, botched abortion; dirty instruments had been used.' And Bill said 'No, no, not Beck.' I said, 'No, no, no, not my Becky. Oh my God, not Beck.'

I told Bill that I did not want people talking about Becky. We grew up in a small community. Everybody idolized us. We were the perfect couple — the perfect family. I didn't want people to call her a whore. We agreed to say that Beck died of pneumonia. It wasn't a lie. The death certificate listed the cause of death as septic

in Texas, but in every state. It was a stunning and momentous development in the struggle for women's equality.

The Supreme Court's ruling meant that government must remain neutral in a woman's decision about whether or not to have an abortion. Roe was a careful compromise, recognizing a woman's constitutional right to choose abortion up to fetal viability — when the fetus is capable of living outside the womb — as

Becky Bell

abortion with pneumonia.

Right before the funeral, the minister came over and knelt down in front of us. He said, 'Why don't you tell the truth so you can hold your head up in the community? You can help other people. You can help yourself and avoid living a lie.' I thought the truth would come out someday and so we agreed.

At the funeral, the minister said that Becky had been pregnant and had died as a result. I bowed my head. I couldn't look at anybody.

Billy asked if he could close the casket. He stood beside Beck and stroked her head. He said, 'Beck, nobody will ever hurt you again.' And that was it.

Bill and I didn't care whether we lived or not. I didn't know where Billy was half the time. One day, about six months later, Billy said to me, 'You're not my mom anymore. You lay and you cry and the house is dark. You don't cook. No one comes over. What about me?' Our son needed us. It woke us up.

One day, we got a letter from Peter Jennings. He wanted us to be on the news to talk about Becky, who was the first teenager known to die because of a parental consent law. I said, 'Bill, what's parental consent?' He didn't know either. That's when we started looking into what happened to Becky.

Bill and I talked to Becky's friends and learned that she had sought an abortion at Planned Parenthood. They told Becky that they would help her but that because she was a minor, she had to get a parent's permission to comply with Indiana law. If she couldn't talk to a parent, she could seek permission from a judge. Becky told the counselor, 'If I can't tell

my mom and dad, how can I tell the judge?' They also told Becky that she could get a safe and legal abortion in Kentucky without telling her parents. But there was no way that Becky could get to Kentucky without us suspecting something.

Becky told the Planned Parenthood counselor that she had hoped that the boy who got her pregnant would marry her, but he didn't want her in his life anymore. After Becky died, some of his ex-girl-friends told us that the boy's standard line was that he was sterile because he had had the mumps. Those girls believed him, and Becky must have believed him.

Bill and I decided to speak out; we thought we could prevent other girls from dying. We appeared on "60 Minutes." The anti-choice crowd came after us. They followed us. There would be crowds of people with their fetuses in a bottle, and some would say that Becky didn't die the way we said she did. They loosened the lug nuts on our car. In Arkansas, they shot a hole in the building where we were speaking. They cared more about a fetus than about my daughter. I thought, 'I'm not afraid of anybody, because my daughter is dead and you can't hurt me anymore.'

People ask me what I would have done if Becky had told me the truth. I would have been mad, and I would have said, 'Becky, you just ruined your life. What are the neighbors going to think?' That would have been my first reaction because that's who I am. But then I would have asked her, 'Beck, do you want to get married? Have a baby? Have an abortion? What do you want? What can you live with, hon?' We would have worked it out. But I never got the chance.

well as the state's interest in protecting potential life after viability except when the woman's health or life

was at stake. Beyond that state interest, Roe *recognized that the abortion decision belonged to the woman*

with her doctor — not to government or politicians.

Roe *changed the course of history and women's lives, restoring their dignity, improving their health,*

MARY CONLEY

Mary Conley is a 38-year-old writer who lives on the East Coast. She was 22 and single when she became pregnant. Like many women, Mary did not want to bring a child into the world at a time when she wasn't ready financially or emotionally to be a mother. She had a safe, legal abortion but had to face an angry thicket of protestors at the clinic. Today, Mary is an outspoken advocate of a woman's freedom to choose.

After college, I started working in restaurants in my hometown and eventually couldn't go anywhere in the city without running into people who knew me. I felt trapped. On top of that, my boyfriend had just dumped me at Christmas. I wanted to start over in a city where no one knew me. I was an aspiring writer, and I had dreams of becoming the next Tennessee Williams or maybe Eudora Welty. So I moved to New Orleans to write the great American novel.

On my way to New Orleans, I visited old family friends. We celebrated one brother's 30th birthday and partied a lot. I ended up sleeping with the birthday boy without using any birth control. I remember telling him, 'If anything happens, don't worry about it. I'll take care of it.' Those words would come back to haunt me.

I took the bus to New Orleans, rolled my bags across the French Quarter, and got a room in a youth hostel. Within 24 hours, I found work as a waitress. One day while dressing for work, I glanced at my breasts in the mirror and realized that they were bigger and more sensitive than usual. I grabbed my calendar and counted back to the day I had sex. It was on the 13th day of my menstrual cycle. My heart sank.

In those days, there were no early home pregnancy tests. So I spent the next several weeks until I could be tested telling myself I wasn't pregnant. I couldn't deal with the thought. But my skin was really oily, my fingernails became so hard I could climb mountains with them, and my breasts were so sensitive that I couldn't wear a shirt without being in pain.

Finally, I was able to get tested at the neighborhood clinic. The doctor came in and said, 'Well, let's see how far along you are.' He didn't even bother to tell me I was pregnant. I bolted as upright as one can while in stirrups and said, 'I'm pregnant?!' I told him that there was no way that I could have a baby. In those days, nobody I knew was a single mom. And I wasn't going to be the first.

I had always been a good kid. I took honors courses, graduated early from high school, and went to a good college. My parents thought I was destined for great things.

and enabling them to participate more fully in society. Women who sought to terminate their pregnancies

no longer had to endure the indignities, degradation and danger of back-alley abortions. Roe exonerated

those who risked their lives trying to make responsible reproductive health decisions. And Roe meant

that future generations of women could make their own reproductive decisions about pregnancy,

I couldn't be pregnant — I couldn't do that to my family. My parents never hit or punished us — seeing their disappointment was enough of a punishment. To come home pregnant would have been the supreme disappointment.

I was afraid to tell the guy in question for fear that he would insist on marrying me. He was a fine person, but he was a farm boy and I was a city girl, and I knew that we wouldn't make a good couple. So I ended up at a pay phone on a corner in the French Quarter crying long-distance to old friends. I had finally gotten what I wanted: I was totally alone.

Getting pregnant was a mistake, and I wanted to correct my mistake as quickly as possible. I scheduled the abortion for that Saturday.

The next day, I told a co-worker that I was pregnant. She said, 'Oh my God. I think I am, too.' She took a pregnancy test and found out she was right. She scheduled her abortion for the same morning as mine.

On the appointed day, I packed maxipads, a sweater and socks as they'd told me to do. I walked to the clinic, which was only six blocks from my new apartment. As I got closer, I could see picket signs. Men and women were pushing baby carriages and handing out pamphlets with pictures of fetuses on them. As I scooted past them, one protestor yelled at me, 'Think about Jesus before you do that.' I said, 'Jesus and I are fine on this.'

Safely inside, I filled out some forms and took a seat in the waiting room. Saturday morning cartoons were blaring on the TV, and Frank Sinatra was crooning on the stereo, but you could still hear the protestors chanting 'Our Fathers,' saying rosaries, and singing hymns. It was torture to sit through. Their righteousness made me angry. How did they know what we were going through? How could they judge us?

My co-worker came in with her boyfriend and her roommate. They had more trouble getting through than I did. The crowd had swelled and was blocking the entrance. Finally, her boyfriend pushed through and pulled her inside. She was crying hysterically. We tried to calm her down, which gave me something to focus on besides my abortion. But the protestors' words would pierce through every time the door opened. 'Baby killers!' 'Murderers!' 'They're killing babies in there!' Their words were calculated to make us feel worse. I would learn later

childbirth, adoption and abortion.

But after a quarter century of legal abortion, the promise of Roe *remains unfulfilled. Although the freedom to choose endures as a legal right, anti-choice activism and subsequent Supreme Court decisions have increased government regulation of abortion and made abortion less accessible.*

Mary Conley

questions, and I am ready for them.

that my co-worker's roommate had gone home and returned with her gun in her purse — in case of trouble when we left. Fortunately, there was none.

We were taken to another room to watch a film about the procedure. Then we changed into gowns, and went one at a time into the operating room. The nurse held my hand and talked so sweetly to me that I started to cry. 'If the doctor sees you crying,' she said, 'he's not going to do this for you because he's going to think that you really don't want this.' I swallowed my tears. The doctor came in and began the procedure. I felt some tugging and heard the sounds they told us to expect, and then, in minutes, it was over. When I left, the nurse said, 'I don't want to see you back here for this again.' And I said, 'You don't have to worry about that.'

Many of the women having abortions that day were married women with children. That surprised me. I always thought abortion was a single woman thing to do, but there are women who have families as big as they can afford and that's it. Each of us in our own way was taking responsibility for our lives and for our families.

A child is the rest of your life. It's every thought you'll ever have, every breath you'll ever take. Having a child can be the most wonderful thing — if you're in a position to be a mom. I would love to have a child now if I could find the right man to be the father. At the time, I was afraid that if I continued the pregnancy, I would make that child bear the brunt of my frustration about putting my life on hold. That was not the kind of mother I wanted to be. I wanted to be like my mom, who had all the time in the world for me. Her children were her greatest joy. There was no question that I was wanted and loved.

To this day, I wear a bracelet inscribed with the name of Becky Bell, the girl who died as a result of a parental consent law. I will wear the bracelet every day until those laws are repealed. The bracelet always provokes questions, and I am ready for them. There's absolutely no part of this debate that I will back down from. Women who have benefitted from the freedom to choose have got to stand up for it — to save it for women who someday will need it like we once did. We owe it to the women who died from illegal abortions and the women who fought to make abortion legal. I'm determined to help keep us from going back to the bad old days when women paid for unplanned pregnancies with their lives.

Anti-choice forces mobilized immediately after Roe *and executed a comprehensive political and legal strategy. They lobbied Congress to pass a constitutional amendment criminalizing abortion and, after failing to muster the necessary votes, promoted a more successful strategy of restricting reproductive choice for America's most vulnerable women. In 1976, for example, Congress passed the Hyde Amendment, which*

KRISTA REUBER

Krista Reuber is a 28-year-old Connecticut native with a master's degree in public health. She has worked with several nonprofit organizations to improve the health of women and children. Krista recently relocated to Venice, CA, where she works as a personal trainer and fitness model and hopes to re-enter the public health field.

When Krista became pregnant as a senior in high school, she was fortunate to be able to involve her parents in her decision about whether or not to have an abortion. What Krista's parents couldn't protect her from was the crowd of menacing protestors outside the clinic.

M y mother suspected I was pregnant even before I did. She noticed that I was run-down and tired, vomiting frequently and even more moody than my usual teenage state. As I was getting ready for school, she asked me if I might be pregnant. I was surprised and doubtful of her diagnosis, but I admitted that I had been sexually active for six months.

My mother always stressed the importance of communication and urged me to be open with her. When I was 12, we attended mother/daughter human sexuality seminars. Although she did not condone becoming sexually active at a young age, I knew that she wanted me to protect myself if I did choose to have sex. My boyfriend and I made an effort to use birth control, but we had unprotected sex several times.

My mother offered to bring my urine sample to a women's health clinic in Hartford while I was at school in our nearby suburban town. She learned later that day that my test results were positive and called me with the news at my after-school job at a shoe store. Positive. . . pregnant . . . me?! Even with my symptoms, I could not believe this was happening. I worked that afternoon in a state of shock.

When I got home, my mother met me at the door with a hug and suggested that we discuss my options with my boyfriend at dinner the next evening. My parents stressed all the lost opportunities I would have; early motherhood would mean postponing my plans for college, putting my career on hold, restricting my travel, and placing a strain on me financially. My boyfriend, who was planning to attend a prestigious university on an athletic scholarship, echoed those sentiments. He felt that neither of us was ready to accept the responsibilities of parenthood. They all made it clear, however, that it was my decision and that they would support me no matter what I chose.

From an analytical standpoint, all of this made sense. I knew that I wasn't ready for motherhood. Still, I longed to know what the experience was all about. How would it

prohibits Medicaid funding for abortion for low-income women except in cases of rape and incest and when the woman's life is at stake. In 1980, the Supreme Court upheld the policy, ruling in Harris v. McRae *that government is not required to provide funding for abortion services.*

The same year, opponents of choice demonstrated their political clout by helping elect a President who

feel to have my body change so dramatically? What would the baby look like? What would it be like to have someone so dependent on me? After several days of emotional turmoil, I gained some clarity. I decided that it would not be fair to bring a child into the world if I was not ready to care for it in all the ways that it needed and deserved. Terminating the pregnancy was the right thing for me to do at the time.

My mother and boyfriend accompanied me to the clinic for the abortion. As we entered the parking lot we saw a crowd of about 60 men and women holding signs and pamphlets. I was concerned. I had heard about anti-choice groups picketing and bombing women's health clinics. My mother glanced about nervously and told me not to worry — but obviously something was wrong.

I was afraid to get out of the car. When I finally did, a group rushed at me and began shouting, 'Don't do it — don't kill your baby!' and 'You'll regret this for the rest of your life!' My boyfriend used his 6'4" stature to push my mother and me through the swarming crowd and toward the clinic entrance. As I neared the door, a slight man with thinning white hair grabbed my arm and in a raspy voice begged me not to go inside. Terrified, I looked at my boyfriend and noticed his clenched jaw. In one quick motion, he freed me from the man's hold and hurried us through the door.

I was safe, but an emotional wreck. I could see silhouettes of the protestors through the sheer curtains — arms flailing, signs bobbing — and I could hear their muffled chants. My eyes filled with tears — tears of fear and anger. How dare they harass me! How dare they grab me! The decision had been hard enough without this. My mother hugged me and told me how sorry she was about the mob outside. The clinic staff also apologized, but conceded that there was little they could do to make them go away.

By now I was sobbing, and I felt weak and shaky. Fortunately, the stack of forms I had to fill out and the counseling session that I had to attend gave me something else to focus on, and I regained my composure.

The physician who performed the procedure was very nice and apologized about the protestors. He made every effort to comfort me, promising that I would be fine and that later in life when I was ready to have children, I would have a wonderful family.

By the time we left more than three hours later, the protestors had gone. I was so drained that I fell asleep in the car and did not wake up until the next morning. During the days that followed, I grew increasingly enraged at the audacity of the protestors. I believe that the woman — and no one else — has the right to make decisions about her life and health. There is no excuse for the hostile, intimidating behaviors that anti-choice protestors direct toward women seeking abortions. No one should have to go through what I did.

My experience had a profound impact on my life, from my political views to my career choice. Today, I have an unwavering commitment to women's reproductive health care, and I am proudly pro-choice.

packed the federal courts and the Supreme Court with judges opposed to Roe. *State lawmakers enacted abortion restrictions as a vehicle for legal challenges aimed at overturning* Roe *before a Supreme Court grown increasingly hostile to abortion rights.*

Anti-choice Senate candidates rode Ronald Reagan's coattails to victory and control of the U.S. Senate

"If I had lived in a state with a parental consent law,
I would have done anything to avoid
telling them before I was ready."

Jennifer Nye

JENNIFER NYE

Jennifer Nye is a third-year student at a New England law school. She is a graduate of the University of New Hampshire, where she was involved in women's rights and pro-choice advocacy. She is committed to using her law degree to work for social justice, particularly for women's rights.

As a senior in high school in October 1989, Jennifer became pregnant and chose to have an abortion. Like many teens who face an unplanned pregnancy, this was a life-defining moment for her.

I grew up in a small New Hampshire town on the seacoast in a typical middle class family. Both my parents are college graduates who value education and encouraged me to excel academically. It was always a question of where I would go to college, not whether I would go. As a result of this goal-oriented upbringing, I felt as if my self-worth — and my parents' love — depended on my accomplishments. Being an overachiever who made her parents proud was a large part of my identity.

Unfortunately, being a brainy girl doesn't make you very attractive to adolescent boys, and in this respect, high school was difficult for me. There is so much pressure on teen girls to define themselves by their relationships with boys, ignoring their wonderful qualities and skills. I was not immune to this pressure. When a boy started paying attention to me at the end of my junior year, I felt I had arrived.

I had unprotected sex with my boyfriend only once. He told me that if I really loved him, I would have sex without using a condom. I feared that he would leave me or stop loving me if I refused. I knew about birth control — what I lacked was the self-esteem to implement this information. The pressure of having and keeping a boyfriend overwhelmed any judgment I may have had to protect myself.

After we had unprotected sex, I vowed never to do it again. I called a clinic the next day to make an appointment for birth control pills. The clinic worker wouldn't let me make an appointment because I told her there was a possibility I might be pregnant. I know now she could have told me about emergency contraceptives, which are taken the day after unprotected sex to prevent pregnancy. Had she given me this option, I might have been spared the emotionally difficult decisions that surround an unplanned pregnancy.

When I confirmed my pregnancy two weeks later, I knew that I was not ready emotionally, psychologically, or financially to care for a child. At 17, I was mature

in 1980. They held hearings on when life begins and again pushed for a human life amendment that would make abortion illegal. The amendment failed narrowly despite the backing of the Reagan-Bush Administration.

Frustrated by their inability to immediately criminalize abortion, grassroots activists increasingly

enough to know that marrying my boyfriend would only compound the problem, not alleviate it. My boyfriend and I also discussed giving the child up for adoption, but I could not make that decision. Some may say that was selfish of me, but I needed to make the decision that was best for me. I know that, for me, abortion was the right choice.

As important as this decision was, I chose not to involve my parents. I didn't want to hurt them — or risk losing their love. At the time, I felt that their love was conditioned on my being perfect. Getting pregnant seemed like a huge imperfection.

My decision to have an abortion was an informed one. During the three weeks between my initial decision and my abortion, I did a lot of research. This quest for information sometimes proved very painful. One book said that I would get breast cancer if I had an abortion, another said that I would never be able to bear children, and a third stated that the soul of the fetus would come after me and try to kill me. I found all these books in my public library.

Although there were no anti-choice protestors at the clinic the day I had my abortion, I felt assaulted by the intensive media coverage of the anti-choice movement. It seemed that there was an anti-choice activist calling women who had abortions bad, selfish, immoral, and murderers in every newspaper I read or radio station I listened to. How could so many people, who didn't even know me, sit in such harsh judgment? While I never felt guilty about my abortion, the social condemnation made me feel ashamed.

One week after my abortion, I told my parents. My boyfriend was no longer there for me emotionally and I felt that I needed my parents' support. They said how sorry they were that I hadn't been able to come to them beforehand, but that they loved me and supported my decision.

Shortly after I had my abortion, I learned about Becky Bell, a 17-year-old in Indiana who died in 1988 as a result of an illegal abortion. She obtained that abortion to avoid telling her parents about her pregnancy, as required by Indiana law. Like Becky, and perhaps like other young women, loss of parental love and approval was just as powerful a deterrent to involving my parents as the fear of punishment and abuse. If I had lived in a state with a parental consent law, I would have done anything to avoid telling them before I was ready. For this reason, I felt a connection to Becky because she could have been me. The only difference between us was luck and geography. She lived in a state where she had to tell her parents and I did not. She died for her choice. I did not.

This connection made me want to tell my story to help spare other young women Becky Bell's fate and to help ensure that they have access to safe, legal abortion. I was determined that Becky's death, and the deaths of other women from illegal abortions, would not be in vain.

The first time I told my story in public can perhaps be viewed as an accident. I wrote testimony for a state hearing on a proposed mandatory parental involvement bill. I planned to submit my testimony in writing because the prospect of speak-

resorted to harassment, intimidation, arson, bombings and even murder at women's health clinics. The violence ultimately would claim five lives and injure seven others.

Violence at the clinics created a climate of fear and terror that dramatically reduced the availability of abortion services. By 1992, 84 percent of all counties in the United States had no

ing in front of such a large audience was frightening. However, as the hearing progressed, it became apparent that a crucial voice was conspicuously absent — that of young women who faced unplanned pregnancies and chose abortion. After a male teenager spoke in favor of the consent law, saying he represented all New Hampshire teens, I knew my voice had to be heard.

I told the legislature that I wished that abortion did not have to exist. I wished that birth control was 100 percent effective and that everyone who engaged in sexual activity used it. I wished that rape and incest and mistakes did not happen.

I wished that every woman embarked on the long journey of motherhood voluntarily. In short, I wished that humans were perfect. But I told them that humans are not perfect and wishes are not reality. And as long as this is so, all women — regardless of age or where they live — must have the right to safe, legal and accessible abortion.

After speaking, I felt empowered because I knew my voice could make a difference. While we won the fight that day in the legislature, other battles remain. I will continue to play my part in securing the right to choose.

physicians who performed abortions.

Opponents of choice used other tactics to generate public support. In the mid-1980s, they released
The Silent Scream, *a misleading and sensational film that used ultrasound images of fetal life in an*
effort to equate abortion with the murder of a newborn baby. The goal was to shift the abortion debate

ELIZABETH FURSE

U.S. Rep. Elizabeth Furse (D-OR) was raised in South Africa, where she began her public service career by marching against apartheid with her mother, a founder of the South African women's anti-apartheid group Black Sash. Rep. Furse moved to the U.S. as a young woman and eventually settled in Oregon, where she became known for her advocacy on behalf of low-income women, farm workers and Native Americans. Rep. Furse was elected to Congress along with a record number of women lawmakers during the 1992 "Year of the Woman." She is serving her third term.

In 1961, Rep. Furse was a Los Angeles homemaker and mother expecting her third child. She became ill with the measles, which had a devastating effect on the fetus. When Rep. Furse sought to have an abortion, a panel of doctors offered her a cruel choice that no woman should ever have to face.

My husband and I were good and caring parents, and we wanted a large family of four children. By the time I was 25, we had a 3 1/2 year old daughter and a 2 1/2 year old son, and I was pregnant with our third child. In my first trimester, I caught what seemed to be a simple cold. When I developed a very high fever, I was diagnosed with the measles. For an adult, the measles is like a bad case of the flu, but for a fetus, it is a disaster.

My husband was an obstetrician and understood what a profound effect the measles would have on the fetus. Subsequent tests confirmed our worst fears. If I carried my pregnancy to term, our baby would likely be blind, deaf, and severely brain damaged. Everybody we spoke to in the medical community was convinced that the fetus would be severely affected. We were so frightened and so sad as we considered our options.

We were anxious to have more children, but we did not want our child to suffer and to feel such terrible pain. We weighed our responsibility to our unborn child and made the heart-wrenching decision that bearing this child wasn't the responsible thing to do. We decided to seek an abortion.

My obstetrician was sympathetic, but said that he could not help because abortion was illegal and that he and I could be prosecuted and jailed for terminating my pregnancy. At the time, the only way to obtain an abortion legally was if the life of the mother was threatened.

I was absolutely not going to have an illegal abortion, which could be terribly

away from a concern for the woman's health to the fetus.

As the 1980s drew to a close, the anti-choice legal strategy began to pay off. The Supreme Court's 1989 ruling, Webster v. Reproductive Health Services, *marked the first sharp departure from* Roe *and signalled the Court's willingness to allow states greater latitude in restricting abortion. Between*

dangerous. I knew women who went to San Francisco or Mexico, not knowing whether they would come back healthy — or come back at all. In desperation, they were forced to make those horrible, life-threatening choices because abortion, which could have been done simply and safely by licensed physicians, was illegal. My husband had seen so many women with botched abortions who had been dumped on the front lawn of the hospital where he worked. It was a frightening time for women.

My doctor said there was another possibility. Because I have only one kidney, we might be able to persuade a panel of physicians at the hospital to recommend terminating the pregnancy because it placed my life in danger.

We hung our hopes on this chance. My doctor presented my case to the physicians. They were willing to approve the abortion, but only if I had a total hysterectomy so that my life would never again be "threatened" by a pregnancy.

I faced a dreadful choice. I could carry a severely damaged fetus to term or lose my fertility forever. I adored and enjoyed my children and loved the idea of having more. But as someone who loves children, I could not bring a child into the world who was going to be severely damaged. It would not be responsible to do so nor would it be fair to my two little children who also had real needs.

We made a choice — a difficult, painful choice — but one that was right for me and for my family. We chose the abortion — and the hysterectomy that went with it.

All of these deliberations took so long

that I was four months pregnant when they finally did the hysterectomy. The surgery, under general anaesthesia, was a lot more dangerous than an abortion would have been.

We were both very, very sad about our experience — very, very sad. I had my kids to think of, so I got on with life, but it was depressing. One of the most depressing aspects was that somebody else had made a decision for me that I was quite capable of making.

Today, I have a loving husband, two wonderful children and a grandchild who brings me enormous joy. My life is very fulfilling and I look forward, not back. I remain angry, however, that a responsible, loving family was put in that position.

I am a very private person, and I didn't tell anyone outside my family about my experience. I've always been a fighter for choice, but there comes a time when you really have to put yourself on the line. I decided to speak out about my experience to warn people about the dangers if this right is taken away.

For the last several years, anti-choice Members of Congress have been attacking a woman's right to choose. Step by step, they are very effectively chipping away at our basic right. If you are a federal employee, you cannot choose a health insurance plan that covers abortion. The District of Columbia cannot use its own funds to pay for abortions for its low-income residents. And if you are stationed overseas in the military, you cannot have an abortion in a military hospital even if you paid for it with your own money.

1989 and 1992, more than 700 anti-choice bills were introduced in state legislatures.

In 1992, the Supreme Court, in Planned Parenthood v. Casey, *enabled state legislatures to enact even more onerous restrictions. The Court also abandoned* Roe's *strict scrutiny standard in favor of a less protective one that permitted states to impose restrictions as long as they did not unduly burden a*

With these insidious votes — take a little bit of a right here, then a little bit of a right there — pretty soon you're left with a pretty empty right. That is why we must be ever vigilant to ensure that the right to choose is not left in the hands of politicians who know nothing whatsoever about you or your circumstances.

I am also telling my story because I am concerned that young women don't know what it was like when abortion was illegal. And they don't realize that they have to keep fighting to safeguard the right to safe, legal abortion.

I am not afraid to speak out. I am a fighter. I fought against apartheid when I lived in South Africa. I fought for civil rights in the U.S. I'm determined to warn people that a woman's right to choose is not something abstract — it is a very real right — and without it, women will die again from botched abortions.

woman's right to choose. Following Casey, *legislation to make abortion more difficult was introduced in nearly every state.*

These challenges to a woman's freedom to choose galvanized America's pro-choice majority. NARAL developed the "Who Decides?" message that resonated with abortion rights supporters and

SHANNON LEE DAWDY

Shannon Lee Dawdy, 30, is an archaeologist and research associate at the University of New Orleans. She and her husband of four years were excitedly awaiting the birth of their first child in early 1997 when ultrasound testing showed something was terribly wrong with the fetus. Shannon's tragedy was compounded by Louisiana laws that require women to undergo biased counseling and a 24-hour waiting period before having an abortion.

Everything was wonderful for about four months. We went for a routine ultrasound, and seeing our child for the first time made the pregnancy real for me. The baby was moving and, to our untrained eyes, looked normal. When the technician sent us to my ob-gyn for the results, I assumed it was standard procedure. Our ob-gyn, who had been briefed by the radiologist by the time we arrived, said that part of the fetus' skull was missing, a serious problem that might not be correctable. She urged us to consult with a neonatologist and to consider our options, including terminating the pregnancy.

I was in shock. Within one hour, we went from the high of seeing our baby for the first time to the possibility that we might lose it. It was a roller coaster of emotions.

We didn't get much sleep that night. The next day, the neonatologist didn't mince words. He called it anencephaly, a neural tube defect in which the skull doesn't close and brain tissue cannot form normally. He said that these babies, if they are born alive, don't live more than three days. That sealed my decision. Through my tears, I said I would terminate the pregnancy. My husband supported my decision.

I didn't see the point of carrying this child to term and prolonging its suffering. And the thought of delivering a deformed child who didn't have any possibility of life was more than I could bear. I'm a pretty strong person emotionally, but I don't think I could have handled that. I know that some people, because of their religious beliefs, decide to bring these children to term. They see victory in getting the child to live a record 10 days. My religious beliefs don't insist on life at any cost.

What really angers me about the abortion debate is that anti-choice people want to play God with people like me. This was an extremely personal and painful situation, and no one can know what they would do unless confronted with similar circumstances.

I asked the neonatologist to help me as quickly as possible. I was in extraordinary emotional pain and I couldn't begin healing until the pregnancy was over. What's more, since I was four months pregnant, I had to undergo an induced labor abortion, which

reframed the national abortion debate. In 1989, in anticipation of the Webster ruling, and again in 1992 in the months before Casey and the Presidential election, an estimated 500,000 pro-choice Americans marched on Washington to show widespread support for protecting reproductive choice. In 1989, pro-choice organizations mobilized voters and made reproductive choice a deciding factor in the

my name to each item. There were a couple of lines about options for adoption which, of course, was totally irrelevant in my case. It was a nightmare.

When the procedure finally occurred, I had to have the abortion in the labor and delivery area with happy births going on around us. My husband stayed with me during the labor, which lasted the full 18 hours. At 2 a.m., the fetal monitor no longer detected a heartbeat. The contractions had ruptured the connection with the umbilical cord, so the child had already died. At 7:30 a.m., the ordeal was over.

The experience changed me as a person. It made me more sensitive to people and what they might be going through. It also increased my interest in supporting pro-choice legislation. What outrages me is that the Louisiana legislature has passed a raft of anti-choice bills, including a ban on some late-term abortions. They also have made it possible for women who have abortions to sue their doctors up to 10 years after the fact.

The climate here is very anti-choice. I wonder whether it affected my doctor's decision to perform an induced labor abortion rather than a type of abortion known as dilation and extraction, which would have been far less traumatic for me. If the rabid anti-abortionists had their way, I would have brought this child to term. The inhumanity of that attitude just astounds me.

I'm not ready emotionally to get pregnant right now. I'll wait a year or two, and hopefully I'll be in a different environment where I won't have so many reminders of my experience — or of the cruelty of anti-choice laws.

would take 18 hours. I wanted to begin as soon as possible. The doctor understood and made arrangements with my ob-gyn to do the procedure the next day.

But the worst was yet to come. The next morning, my ob-gyn called and said that there had been a misunderstanding. According to Louisiana law, I had to wait 24 hours from the point at which I signed some release forms. The neonatologist and the ob-gyn each thought the other had given me the papers to sign.

At that point I almost had a nervous breakdown. That this nightmare would last another 24 hours was almost more than I could take. I started screaming. I was so hysterical that my husband had to hold me down.

We met with the ob-gyn. She gave us material to read and forms to sign. I was extremely angry, not at her, but at the law and the men who made it. I was supposed to calmly read all this information — anti-choice propaganda, really — and sign

election of two pro-choice Governors.

Abortion rights also became a defining issue in the 1992 presidential election. Pro-choice Americans recognized that the Supreme Court was only one Justice away from overturning Roe *and that voting pro-choice was essential to safeguarding a woman's reproductive freedom.*

Shannon Lee Dawdy

Byllye Avery is a long-time activist for women's health care and the founder of the National Black Women's Health Project, a nonprofit group dedicated to promoting the health of African-American women. She has won numerous awards, including those from the MacArthur Foundation and the Academy of Science Institute of Medicine. She lives in Swarthmore, PA.

Byllye became an activist in the early 1970s, helping women travel from her home state of Florida to New York, which had liberalized its abortion laws. As a widow with two young children, Byllye never thought that she would need an abortion herself. But sometimes the personal and the political converge in unexpected ways.

The second wave of feminism in the 1970s blew a big breath of life into me. I was excited about the new feminism and eager to help women reclaim control over their bodies and their decisions about pregnancy and childbirth. During this time, I was teaching special education to emotionally disturbed children at a hospital in Gainesville, FL. Our unit was very progressive, and several co-workers and I joined forces to send women with unwanted pregnancies to New York State, which had legalized abortion in 1970.

After the Supreme Court's *Roe v. Wade* decision in 1973, we would spend our Saturdays driving women to an abortion clinic in Jacksonville. It was more than an hour away, and we knew that we couldn't keep this up forever. Three of us began to raise funds to open an abortion clinic in Gainesville.

I became pregnant the same year. I was a widow with two small children; my husband had died three years earlier of a massive heart attack. He was 33 years old and only four months away from completing his doctorate.

One weekend, I took the kids to visit a friend in Miami. Who would have thought that I would have the opportunity to meet someone special, let alone have sex? But I did, and of course I didn't have any birth control with me. I ended up pregnant.

I knew there was no way that I could have another child. I already was raising two children alone and it was not easy. I didn't consider myself a single parent — I was a double parent doing the job of both mother and father. I had to make every decision myself, make sure they went for their checkups, get them to football games on time, help them with their homework, and keep food on the table.

Most women know when it is a good time to have a baby and when it is not. For me, there was no question that I would have an abortion. Thankfully, I could have a safe, legal

Pro-choice groups organized, mobilized and turned out voters on Election Day to help elect a pro-choice President. President Clinton, in one of his first official acts, overturned several anti-choice policies of previous administrations. In 1994, Congress enacted a law to protect clinics from anti-choice violence.

These victories led pro-choice Americans to believe that a woman's right to choose was secure. They

one. Even so, knowing what I had to do and then getting up the nerve to do it were two different things. I kept putting it off. My girlfriend pushed me to schedule an appointment, and finally I did.

I made the trip to Jacksonville. Before the procedure, the nurse said, 'You might have all kinds of feelings when it is over, you may cry a lot, and we'll be here to support you.' I did not react that way. Instead, I felt a sense of relief when it was over.

I believe that we have to face the reality of what we are doing. To me, abortion means stopping a potential life. It would be dishonest for me to say that this is not live tissue. When you prevent conception, you are also preventing a potential life. Abortion is an extension of that prevention. That's the way I see it.

The abortion itself did not have a big effect on me. I returned to work and to our plans to open an abortion clinic.

We raised about $16,000 — a lot of money in those days. Each of us took out a $2,000 loan from the credit union and a line of credit at Sears to pay for furniture, and we borrowed the rest from a few individuals. We decorated the clinic with shag carpet, which was the rage back then. We put flowers in the waiting room, and bright posters everywhere. We wanted women to come to a beautiful place.

It was all very exciting and hush-hush because we didn't know whether people would try to stop us. We knew that we could not go to the medical society and ask for help because they had already told the local Planned Parenthood that there was no need for an abortion clinic. When we opened the Gainesville Women's Health Center, the medical society learned about it like everyone else by reading the newspaper.

We weren't afraid of the reaction. Sometimes you don't know what to be afraid of so you don't walk around with fear in the front. We had a real can-do attitude.

We had some hard times. Sometimes we didn't know whether we were going to make payroll. But eventually we broke even.

I soon realized that women not only needed safe abortions, but also services to help them have healthy babies. Five years later, we opened Birthplace, one of the first free-standing birthing centers in Florida. I assisted in more than 100 births. Looking back, it was wonderful to create two health care environments where women could make choices within the full scope of reproduction.

Over time, my interests broadened from abortion to healthy childbearing to black women's health in general. In 1981, I founded the National Black Women's Health Project. My goal was to bring black women together so we could talk about our health, change our lifestyles, and make decisions about needed policy changes.

I have been active in women's health for 25 years. I would like to pass the baton to the younger generation, and I hope that young people will become more deeply involved in reproductive health activism. It's important that they realize how central the right to choose is and how fragile that right is today.

We must not return to the days of back-alley abortions when women risked their lives and when decisions about pregnancy, childbirth and abortion belonged to others.

became complacent, and reproductive choice lost its saliency as a voting issue. The 1994 and 1996 elections placed anti-choice politicians firmly in control of Congress, many state legislatures and Governor's offices.

A refueled anti-choice movement is increasingly reshaping public policy on abortion at the state and federal levels. Anti-choice politicians have dramatically increased the number of laws that restrict

KATE MICHELMAN

Kate Michelman has been a leading voice on behalf of a woman's freedom to choose for more than two decades. President of the National Abortion and Reproductive Rights Action League since 1985, Kate also has served as Executive Director of Planned Parenthood in Harrisburg, PA. In 1994, she was a fellow at the John F. Kennedy School of Government's Institute of Politics at Harvard University. As an educator, Kate developed a model program for working with children with special needs.

In 1970, Kate was a young mother and homemaker when her husband suddenly left her. She learned that she was pregnant shortly after and began a quest for a safe hospital abortion. Her story reveals the indignities and humiliation that women suffered as they sought to make responsible reproductive choices.

I grew up in the 1950s, when the role of women centered around the family. I came from a close family, so I readily accepted that role. Like many women of my generation, I hoped to get married, have children, and own a home.

By 1970, I was married to a man who was pursuing his career as a college professor, and I had had three wonderful daughters in three years. We were struggling financially, but were able to scrape together the down payment on our first home. I hoped to work in the field of child development, but that was for the future. My daughters were my priority. My life was my family.

One night, my husband never came home. I was sure something terrible had happened to him. I called the police, to no avail. The next morning, my husband walked in the door and announced that he was in love with someone else and was leaving me. Then he was gone. It was not a gradual separation. It was a sudden, dramatic break. He also walked out of my daughters' lives.

I was devastated. I was frightened. My self-esteem was destroyed. Suddenly, my world had collapsed. My vision of life had shattered. I was terrified — terrified of being alone. Terrified of having sole responsibility for my daughters. Terrified of having to provide for my family. I was shaken to the core.

My daughters also were hurt. They, too, felt rejected. I was worried they would be permanently scarred. How could I alone provide all they needed and deserved? I felt that I had failed them. I blamed myself for their suffering.

A few weeks later, I discovered I was pregnant again. This news further devastated me.

women's access to abortion. For the first time since Roe, more than one-third of the states are

enforcing three or more abortion restrictions, including mandatory waiting periods, biased counseling

requirements, and parental consent laws.

Anti-choice Members of Congress have used the appropriations process to deny access to abortion

Another child would cause an unmanageable crisis and destroy my family's ability to cope. I felt as if the very survival of my family was at stake.

I alone had to meet my children's every need — financial, emotional and physical. I had no money, job or car. I had to ask friends to drive me to the market. The five-and-dime store refused to give me a charge account to buy school supplies for my children. I couldn't make the mortgage payments, and I had to sell my home and move into a small rental townhouse. My family was forced onto welfare. Facing another pregnancy was more than I could handle.

I never thought that I would have to make the decision about whether or not to have an abortion. I was raised in a Catholic family, and I was a devout Catholic at the time. For many years, I strictly followed the church's teachings. I even believed that using birth control was a sin.

Abortion was a crime. The very word evoked fear and shame. People didn't talk about it, and I couldn't even discuss it with my mother or sister. I was forced to struggle with this decision alone.

Deciding whether or not to have an abortion was one of the most difficult and complex decisions of my life. It challenged every religious, moral and ethical belief I held. I had to weigh and balance the overwhelming moral responsibility to care for, feed and nurture my daughters against my responsibility to the developing life within me.

I had to take responsibility, not only for my own life, but also for the lives of my daughters. In the end, I made what I believe was one of the most moral decisions of my life. I decided to have an abortion.

There were only two ways to have an abortion then — in the back alleys or in the hospital. To have a therapeutic abortion in the hospital, you had to persuade a hospital panel of doctors to grant you one.

to women whose health care is under congressional control, such as federal employees and women in the military. A congressional ban on certain abortion procedures was thwarted only by a presidential veto.

As pro-choice Americans commemorate the 25th anniversary of Roe v. Wade *on January 22, 1998, powerful forces continue to work to undermine* Roe. *Anti-choice leaders also have thwarted*

Kate Michelman

Some women had to prove that their lives were in danger. I had to convince the all-male panel that I was not capable of raising another a child, that I was unfit to be a mother — even though I had three daughters. They asked intimate questions about my life — about my marriage, what kind of wife I was, what kind of mother I was. I felt ashamed and degraded — and more worthless than ever.

The only alternative to a hospital procedure was an illegal abortion. Someone gave me the phone number of an illegal abortionist, which I carried with me at all times. I was prepared to risk my life if I had no other choice.

The hospital panel finally granted me permission to have the abortion. I was relieved. I arranged to have a friend care for my children and went to the hospital. There, I faced one more indignity. A nurse told me they had forgotten about another legal requirement — I had to get the written permission of my husband. I explained that my husband had left me. She said it was the law and that if I did not comply, I could not have the abortion.

It never occurred to me to try to get around this law. I did what I was told. I got dressed and left the hospital to search for the man who had deserted me. It was just one more humiliation.

He gave his permission, and I had the abortion. When I woke up in the recovery room, I was glad that it was over, but I felt such overwhelming loneliness. I felt like a failure. My husband was gone, my family was in turmoil, and I was worried about the future.

I slowly put the pieces of my life together. It took me quite a while to restore my sense of worth and to meet the various obligations and responsibilities of my family. Eventually my daughters and I recovered and moved on. I completed my degree and found part-time work in the field of child development.

My experience with abortion, as well as my work with developmentally disabled children, taught me how important reproductive choices are to a woman's life and to the well-being of her family. That I was forced to consider risking my life in order to make a responsible decision for my family shocked and profoundly changed me.

Roe v. Wade was decided three years after my abortion. It felt like a retroactive pardon of my decision. The ruling from the highest court in the land provided an affirmation that my decision was indeed right.

Within several years of *Roe*, I decided to devote my life's work to ensuring that no woman would ever again have to face the indignities I faced or risk her life when making reproductive choices. Today, women no longer have to endure back-alley abortions. But for the most vulnerable women — the young, the poor, women living in rural communities — the freedom to choose has become virtually a right in name only.

I will continue to make the daily fight to secure a woman's freedom to choose for all women, including my three daughters and their children. It is for them that I persist in this fight. It is for them that I give voice to my story — so that they never have to face the shame, degradation and humiliation that I and countless other women suffered when taking personal responsibility for our lives and for our families.

policies that would make abortion less necessary through serious attention to prevention, including sexuality education and family planning, and healthy childbearing. Until the nation secures policies that promote a full range of reproductive health services, uphold women's rights and strengthen families, Roe *will remain an unfulfilled legacy.*